IT ALL STARTS WITH MARKETING

A Guide to Finding the Perfect Consultant
to Help You Dominate Your Marketplace!

By Paul Conant

Table of Contents

Introduction

Over the past couple decades, I've learned the secrets to successful marketing. Yes, you've probably heard 100 people tell you that by now if you're considering hiring a marketing specialist. Have you wondered what sets those who simply say that and those who actually mean it apart? The final financial result for your business is what ultimately separates the two. However, you'll notice some telltale signs along the way if someone is not going to deliver the promised results. If you want to be sure of your marketing specialist helping you achieve your goals, the individual or firm must meet these criteria:

- They should spend more time listening to you than talking to you.
- They should have an actionable plan that includes personalized tactics and strategies.
- They should offer a realistic time frame and numbers.
- They should use an overall strategy that increases profitability without significantly increasing your work load.

If you've ever hired a marketing specialist, you know from experience that you can see the results and promising signs of success or a lack of those signs quickly. You know the frustration of wasting time and money on a marketer who doesn't know what to do. Their empty promises look great on paper and are encouraging enough to entice you to sign up for their services. However, they wind up being about as helpful as a screen door in a submarine, and your business suffers or remains unchanged as a result.

You can dip an onion and an apple in caramel and put a stick in them. While they will both look like a caramel apple on the outside, you'll know the difference when you bite into them. The same idea is true with marketers. Some have the appearance of knowing what they're doing outwardly but actually do not know much at all. They can coat themselves however they choose. On the inside, they're still onions. I'll teach you how to avoid picking the onions.

My passion is marketing and helping businesses succeed and even exceed their goals if possible. I always promise a realistic evaluation to my clients, and I help them develop realistic goals. The first thing to remember is that marketing is not the same as advertising. Also, tactics and strategies are two very different things even though they're related. This book will help you understand why you need a marketing specialist, what marketing is, why you need to make it a priority and how you can work with someone who will help your business thrive.

Don't waste your time with people who are more than happy to take your money, not listen to you and then disappear when they don't provide what they promised. Use this book to educate yourself, and you'll understand what you need to do and how to work with someone who is smart, knowledgeable and reliable. My goal is to help every business succeed, grow and solve problems through effective marketing.

What is a Marketing Consultant?

Marketing consultants are experienced professionals that can help a business create and execute strategies that will market, or sell, that company's products or services. It's very important to understand that marketing consultants are not just ad agencies or advertising executives. While creating ads and tag lines will be part of a marketing consultant's job, there is much more involved.

A marketing consultant will help a company price, package, distribute and sell their product or service. These things are included in what's known as the "marketing mix," a mixture of ideas and strategies that will advertise the product, but will also take every element of the product into consideration to make it better and more accessible and appealing to the public. Essentially, a marketing consultant must be able to advise their clients on the best way to sell their products and that includes every aspect of that product, not just how it is advertised.

Marketing consultants must be able to bring a lot of skills and knowledge to the table. They must be able to understand the thoughts, actions, and behavior of consumers so that they can understand why consumers buy the things they do. Marketing consultants must be able to understand things such as the targeted demographics for a specific product and then figure out what media outlet is best for reaching that demographic. They must understand what type of marketing that target demographic is going to respond to best and what will drive the consumer to buy the company's product or service.

Along with critical thinking skills, a marketing consultant must be able to think creatively. The world of marketing is one that is always changing and one that consumers can quickly become bored with. Using the same marketing strategy that's been used for millions of companies isn't going to work, because consumers simply won't respond to it. A marketing consultant must be able to think of creative strategies that will interest consumers in the product and get them to eventually buy it.

Marketing consultants can either be proficient and knowledgeable in all areas of marketing, or they may specialize in one certain area of it such as Internet marketing, direct mail, or mobile marketing. Marketing consultants can be a single person or a large firm. Large firms will most likely include things such as web design into their services and they may also have separate departments for client services, production, and distribution. Other marketing consultants have their own business and take care of all these things themselves, or with a small staff. Either way, you shouldn't choose your marketing consultant based on the size of the company they own or work for. You'll need to do some of your own digging and research to decide which marketing consultant is truly best for you and your company.

Why Hire a Marketing Consultant?

When it comes to marketing your company's product there are a few choices that you have. You can do it yourself, you can hire someone full-time to take on the job, or you can hire a marketing consultant. This latter choice is really the only way to go. Yes, that's partly because they bring all the skills, experience and knowledge necessary to do the job correctly, but that really is only part of it. There are so many reasons to hire a marketing consultant and few reasons why you shouldn't.

Just like everything else in your business, marketing comes down to money. The better your marketing campaign is, the more money you are likely to make. While you may think that hiring a marketing consultant will take away from that extra profit because you'll be spending those extra dollars on your consultant, this is absolutely not true. If you take on the giant task of marketing yourself and fail, it will cost your company hundreds and thousands of dollars. When that happens your marketing budget may already be tapped, disallowing you the opportunity to find your mistakes and do it again properly a second time. This is not the only way that marketing consultants will save you money.

If your small business needed to have its roof repaired, would you hire a contractor full-time to stay on with your company in the event that you need roof work done again at some point? Of course not! You'd hire a contractor to take care of the problem and your business would be finished with them once the job was done. If you have another roof problem in the future you'll call them back and arrange for a new job, but there's no need to pay them in the meantime. The same is very true for a marketing consultant.

While hiring a full-time marketing individual or department will allow you to hand over marketing jobs and duties to that person when they arise, that won't be all that often. Once your marketing strategy has been created and implemented, there will be very little for your marketing consultant to do on a day to day basis. While you may have to bring them in once in awhile to adjust marketing strategies and change them slightly, it's certainly not worth bringing someone in full-time. Keeping someone on your payroll permanently will definitely cost you a lot more in the long run than hiring a consultant would.

Another very good reason to hire a marketing consultant is because you are too busy to do it yourself. As the owner of a small business, you're already juggling several balls in the air. Marketing is an enormous area and if you take it on yourself, you're bound to drop one of those balls, either in the marketing department or somewhere else within the company. Also if something gets missed it's going to cost your company money in one form or another.

These are all great reasons to hire a marketing consultant for your small business. But there's also the factor of just bringing in someone new. Every time you ask someone new about their opinion of your business and how it does things, you're going to get a new perspective and will have a new chance to see things from the consumer's point of view. A marketing consultant's opinion will be one of the best ones you'll ever get because they truly understand consumers and what drives them to buy the products that they do. While you may have been doing things the same way for the past year, or even several years, a marketing consultant can show you where you're going wrong and can help you make it right. In short, a marketing consultant's opinion is a very professional and knowledgeable one – and one that can make your company a great deal of money!

The Different Types of Marketing

Before you start compiling your list of marketing consultants and speaking to each of them, there are a few marketing basics that you should be familiar with. This is so that when you first sit down to speak with a marketing consultant you'll be able to do much more than just shrug your shoulders and tell them to "make you money." You should be able to tell them a few things such as which forms of marketing you think will work best for your business. There are many different types of marketing that you can use- here are some of the most common forms.

Print Marketing

Print marketing involves placing your ads and marketing campaigns into newspapers and magazines that are specialized to the type of product you sell. So if you sell fishing tackle, you'll want to run ads in a fishing magazine. If you sell clothes you'll want to choose fashion magazines for your ads. If you are only a local company that doesn't conduct business outside of your state or city you'll want to stick with print media that's in your area so you don't waste time advertising to people that will never use your business. Print marketing has some of the strictest deadlines in the business, because they prepare their publications months ahead of time, and because they need all of the content before their paper or magazine can go to print.

Direct Mail

Direct mail marketing is when you send out brochures, pamphlets, letters, or other marketing materials to a mass group of people at the same time. Many people think that direct mail marketing is a dead form of marketing but that's not necessarily true. There are many instances in which direct mail can be effective, as long as you make sure that you make it personal and not just like another form letter.

TV and Radio

TV and radio are by far considered to be the 'Kings of marketing' and there are many good reasons for it. TV and radio both offer the company an opportunity to reach a huge amount of people in a very short amount of time. Consumers also seem to be more open to this kind of advertising because it doesn't take away from their own life, or what they're doing the moment they see it. TV and radio have also been shown to be especially effective parts of marketing campaigns. However, there are some downsides to using these types of media in your marketing campaign. The first is that they are extremely costly and the second is that they hit a huge group of people so there's no way to ensure that your target demographic audience will be the focus.

Online Marketing

If TV and radio are considered the 'kings' of marketing, then online marketing is definitely the queen.

Billions and billions of dollars are spent every year on Internet marketing because it's becoming the most popular form of media for users. Online marketing includes the best things about TV and radio, such as reaching a huge group of people in a short time, but it's far cheaper and can be more targeted to specific demographic groups. Some of the most popular forms of Internet marketing are pay-per-click advertising, banner advertising, email marketing, video marketing and organic search using SEO techniques. Online marketing is so effective that many companies are starting to turn away from other forms of marketing such as radio, TV and direct mail and focus only on Internet marketing. It's becoming so popular that it's not hard to believe that one day very soon this form of marketing is sure to be called the "King of Marketing.

Things You Should Consider Before Hiring a Marketing Consultant

Before you start making your list of potential marketing consultants there are a few things you have to figure out. You need to know where your business's current marketing plan stands so that you can see any differences in it in the future. You also need to have a few marketing objectives in mind. This will help you determine what kind of marketing consultant you need because they're not all the same.

Here are a few things that you should know about your business and your marketing campaign goals before you talk to any marketing consultants.

Business-to-Business Marketing or Business-to-Consumer Marketing?

This type of marketing is different than the main print, TV, and online forms of marketing that are available. This type of marketing is based on whether you want to market to businesses or consumers. If your company provides IT support to businesses, then you'll want to target your marketing towards businesses. If your business sells makeup you'll want your marketing to target the consumer. If your business involves dealing with both the consumer and other businesses, such as a wedding planning company, then you'll want a little bit of both types of marketing. The marketing consultant you ultimately decide to hire will be based largely on what type of marketing strategy you want to employ.

Type of Marketing You're Most Interested In

You should have at least an idea of the types of marketing that you are most interested in. If there are some types, such as Internet marketing, that you're unsure of, a good marketing consultant will be able to tell you whether or not your business could benefit from that type of marketing. But you need to have at least an idea of whether you want to see your company's name in your local newspaper, if you're looking to make a TV commercial, or if you want to hear your company's name on the radio.

Your Brand

You need to know a little bit about what your company's business brand is. If you don't think your company has a brand, your marketing consultant will help you create and develop one. Your business's brand consists of anything that makes your company who you are and what it is. If your company has a company logo, a tag line, a song, or anything else that sets your company apart and makes someone think "Your Company" every time they hear it- that's all part of your brand. Bring all of that to the table when you speak with any marketing consultant and they'll help get that brand out to the public.

Your Target Market

You should have an idea of who your target market and demographics are so that your consultant can help you zone in on that demographic and design a great marketing campaign that will truly speak to that target. If you're going to be selling anti-aging cream, your target market is probably going to be people in their fifties, sixties, and older. Your consultant can help you narrow that market down to specific genders. Do you sell anti-aging sunscreen that can be used by both sexes? Or are you selling a line of makeup that will probably be enjoyed mostly by women of that age group? You need to have the basic idea so that you can at least give your consultant a place to get started.

Your Budget

You need to know what your budget is before you start talking to a consultant. Marketing campaigns can become pretty costly and different types of campaigns will cost different amounts. You must do your research and find out how much different campaign venues will cost you before you talk to any marketing consultant. It's easy once you're talking to someone to forget about your budget and get caught up in how your campaign will look on television or how it will sound on the radio. But if you can't afford it, then you simply can't afford it. You need to know that before you meet with your marketing consultant so that you can hold your ground and not be swayed by splashy marketing campaigns.

Your Timeline

Just like your budget, this will be something that you will need to discuss with any marketing consultant that you meet. But you still have to think about it before you meet with any consultant. Do you want your marketing campaign to be on its feet and taking off in three months? Six months? Four weeks? You need to have an idea of what timeline will work for your company so that you can pass this onto a marketing consultant. They will then be able to tell you whether or not they'll be able to do it, or whether someone else will be able to suit your needs.

Your Current Staff

Whenever there's a change in a business it affects the entire staff, not just the owner. Consider whether or not your current staff will need to be involved in the new marketing campaign. There is no right answer here, sometimes they need to be and sometimes they don't. But you need to know this before you hire a marketing consultant. If you think your staff will be asked to help with the new marketing campaign, you'll then need to decide whether or not they're equipped to. The chances are that you have the staff you do because you need them to do the job they're already doing. If you need a staff member to help with marketing needs as well, you might have to consider hiring one that is not your consultant, but will work with and help your consultant.

Your Company's Growth

Everybody wants their company to grow. That's probably one of the biggest driving factors in your decision to hire a marketing consultant! But, you do need to consider just how much growth is healthy for your business and how much is too much. Why would a thing like growth ever be 'too much'? Because if you suddenly start receiving hundreds of orders that you're not equipped to handle, your business will soon run into the ground. This is because when you have more demand than you can supply, it will only result in you having to disappoint customers because you won't be able to meet their needs. One bad referral from a customer can be extremely damaging to a small business, and the more customers you disappoint, the more bad press your company is receiving. Growth is definitely a good thing, but too much growth is not. You need to know before you meet with your marketing consultant just how much growth you're looking for.

How Do You Find a Marketing Consultant?

Odds are it will be easy to find several marketing consultants who operate in your area. The real trick will be to choose the right consultant for your specific needs. You need to perform a little research on your potential choices *before* you decide to hire one of them.

Look for small businesses that have marketing ideas that appeal to you. You don't need to go in and directly ask the owner who handles their marketing, but you can look for small signs, such as a marketing company's logo or name inside certain pieces of brochures, pamphlets, or other marketing materials. If you know any of the small businesses in the area and feel comfortable asking, you can ask them outright who does their advertising, or if they hired a consultant, and start your list of names that way.

The Internet is the most budget-friendly way to reach a huge group of people in a short amount of time. For this reason, most marketing consultants today will have a website. So doing a simple search in your browser for 'marketing consultants' is going to yield you a huge listing of results. You can narrow it down even further by adding your location. This is a great way to look for a marketing consultant for your business because consultants often use their own website to show off their marketing and web design skills, and you can really get a feel for what their marketing vision is and how they could work for your small business.

If you're still having trouble finding a good-sized list of names of marketing consultants, you can always check your local Yellow Pages. Just look under "Marketing Design Firms" for your list of names. These names will automatically be narrowed down into consultants that work in your area.

Once you have your list of potential marketing consultants, you can then start calling around and setting up interview times. Have a list of questions ready to ask. These questions will provide more insight than any website ever could and will help ensure that you hire the right person for the job.

Questions to Ask a Marketing Consultant

1. Are you a legitimate independent contractor?

Anyone can set up shop at their personal computer and call themselves a marketing consultant. You want to make sure that you're working with a legitimate operation and that they're a valid business. Make sure that they have a business license and that appear professional with business cards, a website and their own equipment. This isn't just to make sure that you'll be getting professional results. It's also because if the IRS calls into question their independent status, your company could be liable for anything from taxes to employee benefits.

The other risk you run when you don't work with a licensed contractor is that you could be working with someone who is just in between jobs, or who is just looking for something to do to make some money. Should a better opportunity come along, they could just pick up and leave and you will be left stranded.

2. What marketing courses have you taken?

This is an important question. Remember that you don't have to have a degree in marketing to call yourself a marketing consultant. All you really need is a website with an email address or a business card. It's important to make sure that any marketing consultant you use has some educational background in marketing and has paperwork, such as a degree, to prove that. This will let you know that you're dealing with someone who understands both basic and complex marketing strategies, knows how to lay out a full, detailed, and comprehensive marketing plan and knows how to create both the strategies and the implementation devices to reach your consumers and market your business effectively.

3. Can you provide letters of references for work that you've done in the past?

Good marketing consultants know that letters of reference and testimonials are huge in promoting one's business. Because of this, they should always have letters of references on-hand at all times to give you. Many marketing consultants also post testimonials on their website and this can be a good way to find out what people think of them. Be warned that website testimonials can sound a bit promotional and you may get a better feel of what people really think with actual letters of reference.

Independent consultants can also be pre-screened for you by companies that focus on finding consultants and contractors for businesses. These companies can search the consultant's background, employment history and references for you. If you hire one of these companies you will get a list of potential marketing consultants that have already been pre-screened, which could save you a lot of time and effort. These "contracting mills" as they're known, usually charge $100 or more above the fee of the marketing consultant.

4. Can you provide samples of previous work?

Again, anybody can say that they've worked on *thousands* of marketing campaigns. But you need to make sure that your marketing consultant actually has a lot of experience behind them. Make sure that they can show you samples of past marketing plans, presentations and specific marketing campaigns that they have done in the past. Make sure that they've worked on projects that are similar to what you're looking for and what your company needs. Then focus on whether or not you like the samples they provide you with.

5. What's the longest time you've ever worked with one client?

Generally, if a marketing campaign is not working for a company and not yielding expected results, the client will decide to leave that marketing firm or consultant after one year. If a marketing consultant tells you that they can provide ongoing services to ensure that your marketing campaign continues effectively, they should be able to do so for at least two years and should have done this in the past. Otherwise, you could again just be dealing with someone who thinks that marketing is a good way to make some extra cash from home.

6. What is your level of experience?

You will want to make sure that the marketing consultant you hire has the right level of experience to match your business's objectives. If you only have a small marketing vision for your company and you go with a huge national marketing consulting firm, you're going to be charged a price that's way out of your budget and possibly be given a bigger vision than you originally had in mind. If however, you do have a large vision for your marketing campaign, a big firm might be just what you need. Make sure that you choose a marketing consultant that is tailored to your needs and who has the experience to fulfill it. You don't have to shoot past the stars on this one.

7. Have you ever owned and marketed your own business?

It's easy to lay out a marketing plan and hope it works when it's not your money that's on the line. If a marketing consultant has never had a business of their own, then this is the only type of marketing that they know. When a consultant has been through the same experiences and had the same worries as you, they'll understand how it important it is not to waste your money and to make sure you get the desired result. Aside from that, there are some lessons that can only be learned when they're happening to you, such as a poorly executed marketing plan. When a consultant has been through it before, they're going to actually have walked in your shoes and that counts for a lot. Many times the marketing consultant you'll be speaking to will own their own marketing firm, so you'll find that many of them have owned and marketed their own business.

8. What's been the biggest mistake you've made in marketing?

No marketing consultant or marketing plan is perfect. Oversights are bound to be made, things are bound to be forgotten and sometimes things just go wrong. A marketing consultant has made mistakes in the past, no matter who you're talking to, and they should be able to admit to them. Ask them what they learned from their experience.

9. Have you ever hired a marketing firm or consultant?

This isn't a make or break question, but it's good if the marketing consultant has been in your shoes at one time or another. If they've had to hand over the most important information about their business and completely put the reputation of their company in someone else's hands, they'll know how it feels. And, they'll know even more so how important it is that they do a good job for you.

10. What is your sales experience?

Marketing and sales *are* different, but it's good for anyone who does marketing for your company to also have some sales experience. This is for a couple of reasons. The first is because although marketing isn't only about selling, it does involve selling. It's also because when you work in sales, you have a really good chance of understanding consumers, their buying habits, and why they decide to buy certain products over others. That's invaluable knowledge when it comes to marketing.

11. Are you strategy-focused, execution-focused or both?

Some market consultants focus on strategy only. This means that they'll create, develop and lay out a marketing plan that you will be able to execute and follow on your own. For instance, they may give you a marketing plan and tell you where to go for your advertising and how to build a website, but they won't actually do it for you, they'll just lay the groundwork for you to follow. Other marketing consultants are focused more on the execution aspect of marketing and will take over most of the grunt work for you such as creating your website and getting your ad placed in the paper, but they prefer that you have the ideas and strategies before you consult with them. Many times, especially with the world of marketing consultation becoming so competitive, consultants will offer a mix of both.

12. Do you suggest a selling-based method of marketing, or an education-based method of marketing?

This is a very important question. When a marketing consultant is solely focused on selling to the consumer it comes across to the consumer just as that – that the marketing campaign is strictly meant to sell them something. Being able to sell to the consumer *is* definitely important, but you have to give the consumer something of value. In many cases this is education, because it's easy to give to the consumer for free and because the consumer really does get something helpful and useful out of it. If you're selling sporting goods, you'll want to be not only be able to sell a hockey stick to the consumer, but also be able to advise them on which hockey stick would be best for them.

13. How are you going to use my money to reach the right audience, and not waste it on uninterested parties?

This is an important question. While you should be able to tell your marketing consultant the basic demographic and target market that you're trying to reach, they should be able to tell you exactly how they're going to reach that market.

14. How are you going to measure the success of the marketing campaign?

It is important for you to know if your marketing campaign is working. The consultant needs to be able to show you what results you can expect in a certain time frame. Can they promise that you'll increase your profits by 10% in six months and show you how they're going to do that? Do they have graphs and charts showing all of the different milestones and how your company is going to benefit from them? They should.

15. How is the marketing campaign you'll propose going to separate my company from my competitors?

This is a *huge* question! The world of marketing is constantly changing and businesses and marketing experts are always finding new ways to market to the consumer. The exact point of your marketing strategy is to set yourself apart from the competition. If your marketing consultant can't tell you how they're going to do that, then your consumers won't be able to see it either.

16. Why should I use you as my marketing consultant and not your competitors?

It doesn't' really matter what their answer is, as long as they have an answer. First, if they can't tell you what separates from their competitors then you should find someone who can offer you something unique. Second, if a marketing consultant can't tell you what separates them apart from their competitors they won't be able to tell consumers what separates your company apart from the competition either.

17. Do you work alone as a marketing consultant or as part of a team?

There's no real right or wrong answer here, but it is an important question to ask. If you have a large marketing campaign, or are just working with a large marketing firm, your marketing campaign will probably be handed off to a team of marketing consultants. If however, you are working with a private contractor, you'll probably only deal with that one person and that one person alone. Which one is right for your business will depend on the type of marketing you need and who you find suits you best. But you will want to know who else you'll be dealing with if it's not the consultant you're speaking with at the time.

18. How many clients do you work with at one time?

A marketing consultant will need to be juggling many different balls for different clients at the same time; it is how they make their living. But you want to make sure that the consultant doesn't overload themselves with work by taking on too many clients at one time. This will only mean that you get rushed, sloppy work or, no work at all.

19. Will you sign a letter of confidentiality and refrain from working with my competitors while I work with you?

You can't expect a marketing consultant to *never* work with your competitors again after working with you, but you can ask that they don't work with your competitors while they are under contract with you. This can cause a great conflict of interest and can hurt your company's marketing campaign. You want to make sure that any pertinent information to your company stays within your company and that a marketing consultant doesn't share your ideas with your competition.

20. Do you charge your fee by the hour or by the project?

Some marketing consultants will give you a quote for an entire project while others will charge by the hour. Neither is the right or wrong answer, but you do need to consider a few things before you decide which one is going to be best for your business.

When marketing consultants charge by the project, you run the risk of having the project turn in another direction, which could mean that you won't get your money's worth in the end. Generally, it's best to get a quote for the entire project when the project isn't very complicated. You should also make sure that milestones are clearly outlined. Hourly fees are generally more appropriate if you don't want to hire the marketing consultant full-time, or if they're just filling in for your regular marketing department. When you're being charged by the hour you need to make sure that you're given regular time sheets and invoices that state exactly how much time was spent on one area of the project, what exactly was accomplished during that time and their exact rate for the time spent on that area.

21. Do you have a reasonable rate for your services?

Notice that this is not if they have the *cheapest* rate; it's the most reasonable rate that you're looking for. In fact, you should be wary of any marketing consultant that charges too low for their services. A consultant's time is precious and the only way they make money is through the projects that they do. Therefore, they have to charge enough to live off. If a marketing consultant is charging a price that is just way too low, they may be having a hard time getting clientele, or they may not be a marketing consultant at all. There will be more on the average rates of marketing consultants later on but make sure that you do some research initially and get a good comparison of what marketing consultants in your area are charging. You'll at least get a good feel for what the average is so you will be able to make an informed decision.

22. Will milestones and payment terms be included in the final contract?

You always want to make sure that your marketing consultant will be able to tell you when you can expect certain areas of the project to be completed. They should also be able to give you a schedule of when your website will be up, when certain things will be added to it, when your marketing plan will be prepared and other large milestones of the project. It can be difficult sometimes to know exactly what will need to be done and how long those things will take at the very beginning of the project, especially if the marketing campaign is going to be a long and complicated one. In these cases, it's fine if the marketing consultant can't give you an exact timeline upfront. But make sure they can at least state when they'll be finished and a few basics of how they're going to start getting there.

23. Do you have a good rapport with the marketing consultant?

This of course, is a question that you'll ask yourself and not the consultant, but it is something to consider the entire time you're talking to any consultant. Look past whether or not the marketing consultant is being courteous and polite and look to see if you really 'click' with them. Your marketing consultant will need to have a pretty good idea of your personality in order to achieve your marketing goals and you need to have a pretty good idea of theirs in order to understand and appreciate their concepts. Make sure that it's easy to talk to the marketing consultant and that the rapport between the two of you is good, even during that first conversation.

The Price of a Marketing Consultant

Once you've whittled down your list to a few marketing consultants you will want to consider the price. Price will probably be major factor when it comes to choosing a specific consultant. So, what exactly can you expect to pay for a marketing consultant? The tricky thing about marketing consultants is that none of them really come right out and tell you how much they cost. Because of this you will have to get an estimate from the consultant on your own. Internet marketing has changed the costs and fees of marketing consultants. There are so many different tactics that you can use to market your business online that many consultants base their fees on a number of different factors.

Marketing consultants often have a project-based fee for SEO services such as optimizing your website for search engines and getting the word out about your company's website. When a marketing consultant charges a project-based fee they will generally outline in detail what they will do for your online marketing campaign and what it will cost them to do it. What the fee ends up being will be completely dependent on how large the project is and how detailed the consultant's execution plan is.

Other marketing consultants like to work on a contract-based price. This means that they'll generally have different packages available that outline different services provided for different prices. While this can allow you to pick a package that may work for you, it also won't give you the opportunity to have a customized marketing plan tailored to your company. If the consultant offers the services you need within a package this type of consultant may be all you need and can be a great way to get a good price on what you're looking for.

Many good marketing consultants will charge a monthly retainer basis for their Internet marketing efforts. Within this monthly fee there will be an outline of what you'll receive, what your Internet marketing will involve during every month, and what maintenance will be done to your website, blog or Internet ads over that time. Other marketing consultants use a newer system that is based on page rank or on website traffic. This can be a great benefit to your company because you'll only pay directly based on the results that you get. It's not usually a good idea to use a marketing consultant that solely uses this payment method, as it may mean that you're getting little else in the way of advice or marketing support, but if you're looking solely at the online marketing aspect of your company it can be a great way to save money.

Marketing consultation services that include other aspects of marketing, rather than just your online appearance, will usually be based either on an hourly fee, or a monthly retainer. Fees between different consultants and marketing firms vary greatly. You can expect to pay anywhere from $40 - $100 an hour for consultation services and anywhere from $400 - $1,000 a month when paying on a retainer.

What to Look for When Signing the Final Contract

After you've chosen the marketing consultant that's right for you and talked to them in detail about the price, make sure that they draw up a contract that will outline the services you'll be receiving. Before you sign any contract read it over carefully. Here are a few things you want to look for when it comes time to sign that contract:

- Make sure that the basics are included, such as what will be done during your marketing campaign regarding different mediums and what they will cost.
- Make sure that the contract includes the different milestones so that you can measure where your company is within the marketing campaign and whether or not your consultant is getting things accomplished in a timely manner.
- Look to see that all fees are fully outlined so that you won't be surprised with additional fees and costs when the project is finished.
- Make sure that any payment arrangements and dates are fully outlined within the contract.

Questions to Ask Any Marketing Consultant

- ❑ Are you a legitimate independent contractor?

- ❑ What marketing courses have you taken?

- ❑ Can you provide letters of reference for work you've done in the past?

- ❑ Can you provide samples of previous work?

- ❑ What's the longest time you've ever worked with one client?

- ❑ What is your level of experience?

- ❑ Have you ever owned and marketed your own business?

- ❑ What's been the biggest mistake you've made in marketing?

- ❑ Have you ever hired a marketing firm or consultant?

- ❑ What is your sales experience?

- ❑ Are you strategy-focused, execution-focused or both?

- ❑ Do you suggest a selling-based method of marketing or an education-based method of marketing?

- ❑ How are you going to use my money to reach the right audience and not waste it on uninterested parties?

- ❑ How are you going to measure the success of the marketing campaign?

- ❑ How is the marketing campaign you'll propose going to separate me from my competitors?

- ❑ Why should I use you as my marketing consultant and not your competitors?

- ❑ Do you work alone as a marketing consultant or as part of a team?

- ❑ How many clients do you work with at one time?

- ❑ Will you sign a letter of confidentiality and refrain from working with my competitors while working with me?

- ❑ Do you charge your fee by the hour or by the project?

- ❑ Do you have a reasonable rate for your services?

- ❑ Will milestones and payment terms be included in the final contract?

- ❑ Do you have a good rapport with the marketing consultant?

Conclusion

Now that you know the basics of hiring marketing professionals, it is important to put your critical thinking and analyzing skills to use. One critical step toward hiring the right marketer is looking at consultants' suggestions.

What do the consultants' suggestions say to you? This is an important question to ask yourself, and you should break it down into several subcategories. When you analyze the suggestions closely, your answers will become clearer. Ask yourself these important questions when you're reviewing consultants' suggestions.

Do I really need this? To determine if you need something, think about what would happen if you have it. It's probably something that they promised would be great, right? Now think about what would happen if you don't have it. Will you lose anything? Will it make much of a difference at all? Think carefully and look ahead to determine what is necessary and what is not.

Will this help solve a problem? If something won't help you solve a problem, this should raise a small red flag. It likely isn't necessary if it doesn't work toward a problem's solution. If you find that none of the suggestions solve a problem, then you're looking at a huge red flag waving in your face. Every tactic should be part of an overall strategy that solves one or more problems.

What is the return on investment? There must be a reasonable ROI for every component. This goes along with determining whether something is essential or not. If you can survive without something and it offers little ROI, it may be time to eliminate that item or alter it.

Can I solve this problem on my own? Every business has problems, and every business has its own set of unique problems. Only you can determine if your unique problems can be solved without the help of a professional. When the solutions offered give you little to no ROI or benefit and do not clearly solve a problem, you should either keep looking or see if you can solve the problem yourself. In most cases, the problem is that you're trying to work with the wrong person.

Is this marketer right for my company? Every new or fly-by-night marketer will assure you that he or she was *made* for your business. Be wary of people who are over-eager about getting your money upfront. Opt for experience, personalized success plans and actionable goals over empty promises and platitudes. As we covered in the introduction, be sure the marketer you work with spends more time listening to you.

Remember that marketing is not advertising.

I hope that this book helps you make the right choice in hiring a marketing professional, and I hope you see your business succeed because of it. My passion is success, and I enjoy watching business owners thrive from the information that I am happy to share. Please feel free to reach out to me and share your own success story in the near future.

Contact me for assistance at:

Gizoom.com